# Trouble in the Diocese

# Trouble in the Diocese

DAVID CRAIG

RESOURCE *Publications* · Eugene, Oregon

TROUBLE IN THE DIOCESE

Resource Publications
An Imprint of Wipf and Stock Publishers
199 W. 8th Ave., Suite 3
Eugene, OR 97401

www.wipfandstock.com

ISBN 13: 978-1-4982-0131-5

Manufactured in the U.S.A.                     08/01/2014

"I want to tell you something. What is it that I expect?
I want a mess. I want trouble in the dioceses!
I want to get rid of the mundane."

—POPE FRANCIS I

# CONTENTS

THE APPRENTICE
# PHASE ONE

## INUIT INTROIT

Like hawks, outside of time,
perched on the limbs of the seasons,
the Apprentice passes tucked
Victorian houses; a little boy,
shovels away from his dad, can't lift
what he has gathered, falls to his knees.

His father doesn't notice.
Perhaps he, too, feels it, the night:
rows of sprigs, pin feathers,
sprouting neatly up his back.

He'll want to move away
from the warmth, become apprentice
to frozen planets, to Rilke's
laundry woman.

He'll want to walk dark, snowy fields,
penknife in hand—have it out with badgers.
He'll rip rural mail boxes from their stems,
line them up in front of his cold, broken hearth.
Windows open, he'll hang a bell
around his neck, wait for his ancestors.

# COME, NEGAGFOK

with your furtive cheeks, write in branches,
moonlight ripping the steady lake.

Beneath old ones, tributaries of bark,
the Apprentice leaps from rock to rock,
heaves huge stones into the water.
He listens for the dunking, walks home.

Come, Lord of Purest Grotesquery:
two boot dances in high snow—
shouts which fade
as they cross an open field.

Oh, he knows: the clouds will answer
as they always have, raking the earth
with their iron bars, their tiny voices.

But who has time for them?
The Apprentice chooses the counter-cultural:
complete futility—Cheetoes, hooded,
in front of his cold TV, opened windows,
GREEN ACRES or the cracking of pads,
high school football.

## CHRISTMAS WITH ED AND
## THE REMOTE CONTROL

It's dark now, and the apartment
below his, vacant. On TV, every local high school choir,
"A Child's Christmas in Wales,"
three Scrooge and Marleys,
a flock of *It's a Wonderful Life*s and
*Miracles on 34th Street*,
both in faded color and black and white;
Pavarotti, in costume,
and then, on another channel, in tux;
Loretta Swit in Germany
and Florida versus UCLA—off.

The Apprentice is, at last, alone,
outside—with a solitude to match the season.
Ed barks in the distance;
the apprentice claps his deerskin mitts,
listens to the echoes as his breath climbs
the ladders of Jacob. The cold stings his thighs—
nothing but sharp, pilgrim stars
to steer the weather by.

His nose is the next to burn.

There is no escape. He must return
to his small rooms; paint a number on each
white wall, so he can live where he is:
5, 7, #.

This is no life for the weary.

From his cot he hears a clock ticking,
feels himself age, his hair grow in the dark.
Alert to nothing, like a ball of snakes,
he sits in the ugly Christian wait.

## THE APPRENTICE, AMAZED
(CHRISTMAS)

Oh, for the holiness which eyes the needle,
all the space it leaves in a wine glass!

Everywhere in his life, people are leaving—
except for the crowded department store
downtown, where chandeliers
glisten in fins of light against the ceiling—
all that holiday cheer, grunting below.

Inside his small fridge—this is what there is:
salami, a cold orange with its incredible juices.

Who would have thought life
was going to contain that!

ல ல ல ல

The Apprentice uses lipstick
to draw all over his face.

## THE APPRENTICE REJOICES

Verily, spring hath come,
and there is goodness in the land.
Everywhere snows recede,
everywhere, the sound of running water.

Our little sisters, the plants,
bustle over unmade beds, morning.
Mice stretch in the fields.
(Their little couches are dusty
from the long winter.)
People start going to church,
everyone walking carefully over the earth
as if it were made
of rice paper.

Everybody is Japanese this morning!
Everybody, bowing
with so much deference—
trying to make what lasts
last.

## THE APPRENTICE AND MONSIEUR L'AMOUR

What about the little tubers
that braille rocks, searching each seam
for meaning, a new age? What about them?
Do you think they go on as if nothing has happened,
some kind of cow in the brown earth?

Look, they are as abuzz as icy water
dripping from the eves, as an algebra book
leafing the road.

Every earthly thing rejoiced with you
when you got new tires on your car.
And why not? The planet is more than dirt.
It's true. Everything has already happened!
All you have to do is be still,
put on some clothes, wait to fill them.

Monsieur L'Amour, send yourself some flowers,
hang out on your stoop. Your life
will come visit you on Thursday,
even before your trip to the corner store,
with its colorful packaging, exotic peoples.

## THE APPRENTICE FINDS HIS PLACE

Roses, bobbing, compete: "yup, yupping"
their separate ways. Next to the house
in yellow overcoats, each could be Columbo,
musing, waving its arms.

The Apprentice stands before them,
mimics the wind, the ocean.
He is, at last, Cuchulain, sword in hand,
fighting in fits, his destiny.

But no. These delicate stems, he sees,
are from a different world—
the curve of petal, the come-hither poses. . . .

Up the street, a squirrel rips up
someone's archetypal tree lawn.
The beast restoreth the Apprentice's soul,
leadeth him to stilly waters: the taking, the tearing,
the hundreds and hundreds of tiny teeth.

Nothing is as it seems.
The lawn's ways are not the squirrel's,
and the whole nameless thing rides on the night.

# ON THE CORNER OF HOLLYWOOD AND TIME

Your friend, The End, comes every day:
doorbells and flowers.
He eats your grass, spackles your chimney.
Let him. He is your guest.

Invite him to sit on the porch
to share your melon, spit the seeds.
Barefoot, the two of you
can become halls of angry voices.

Hold your ground, tell him that the red razor
scratches you where you itch.

He'll try a longer face,
tell you the radical laws of departure
are everywhere in evidence,
everywhere a bus stops
on the corner of Hollywood
and time.

Join in the fun.
Tell him that half the passengers there
are dead, but to ignore them;
there is little they can say.

## THE APPRENTICE SEES HIMSELF
## IN THE SUNSET

The lepers grew excited
beneath his window this morning,
danced like Carmen Miranda,
or a band at the Holiday Inn.

Almost immediately, he had a vision
on Third Street, a pietà:
Mother Teresa holding Jimmy Swaggart.
Some kids, off to the left, laughing,
and he heard the sound of a basketball
settling, for a second, in the chain net,
while the sky seemed
like some fragile instrument
made entirely of glass.

The Apprentice wants to start over,
as flowers spring up like earnest
Broadway farm girls, singing "Kumbaya."
They want to buy the world a Coke.

So he decides, grows out all his hairs,
works on his cross-over, sticks
needles in his neck like Alan Iverson.

Why be surprised at this?
Breasts start out high, end up low.
It happens to everybody.

The Apprentice thinks
it's this business of dying:
the cough that won't go away.
He could turn his head, get checked
for prostate cancer.

There's no privacy where he's going.

## LOBSTER EXIT

It probably IS enough
to say one's sorry,
like Scriabin, to regret our claws,
to hold them in shame
behind our backs; to feel,
as the front of our chair is removed,
the depths of our plated natures;
to feel the grace, the mud we flop in,
to warm to garbage.
It's probably enough to feel
the cold blood pulse at our throats,
to crawl self-consciously
across the floor with that slight
side-to-side motion,
to hear the tac-tac sounds
our claws make on the tiles
as people, embarrassed, move chairs
to make way.
It's probably good to see
an antenna occasionally bob before us
as we try to hold up a good front,
march boldly through our secretions
toward the door.

# THE APPRENTICE CONSIDERS FLEAS

The flea on your cot at night
has such tiny feet!
He treks in moonlight
across white dunes.
The buzz of his feelers
occupies all of his attention.
He seldom gives a thought
for his brother who is in Timbuktu
or for the rice on the kitchen floor.

And the moon! It is there
and bathes him is such light!
He sees himself as Donne's chapel,
walled in jet. Call him the Duke,
the Ayatollah, his will,
hard as an abandoned button.

This world depends on him,
he knows this.
He has to be where he is:
his step into
his step.

Siphonaptera,
he has a barb-ed mouth,
speaks many languages,
but who could listen
to him tear himself?

There is no loneliness like his!
Not in all the world!

# THE APPRENTICE SINGS A CAPPELLA

If you want the truth
you must look for it.
It's that simple.
If it's there, it will stick a foot out
as you try to pass in the diner.
He will hold his side
laughing as you fall,
like an insurance salesman
from Nebraska.

It will be more than you expected.

But then, of course,
you must decide
what you're going to do with him.
He might follow you into a Deli,
say something about the Jews.
You can just picture him
down on the corner with the boys,
trying to fit in over the evening fire,
with his wide-open polyester suit,
his white belt.

He'll try to sing the bass part,
completely destroy the harmony.

No sir,
you won't be able to take him anywhere.

# THE APPRENTICE PROPHESIES

It's your small, flat-black porch rail
in sunlight, the matching mailbox.
It's the house brick, texture and grain.
You'll be struck dumb by the ordinary,
and everything will start to matter:
what shirt you put on,
how to pronounce your name.

You'll start helping dogs across the street,
being careful not to cycle over worms after rain.
You and the whole neighborhood,
everyone with quick, uncertain wheels,
hand brakes and balance.
You'll come home hours later,
muddy, but happy.

You'll keep waiting for it to end.

## THE APPRENTICE CONSIDERS
## HIS ADDICTION

The Apprentice is as slick as Vermont maple.
After a shower he greases his hair back,
checks his aquiline nose.

He makes cameo appearances at 7-11s,
eats little powdered donuts
in the back of the store,
gets the white stuff of wisdom
on his beard.

He is your brother, mother;
He is the socks in your drawer:
a sprawl of ganglia, nerve-endings,
and he will go out with your daughter.

And so, if on the street,
he offers you one of his marshmallows,
eat quickly through the pale skin,
catch the gooey center
where the mercury is pure.
There you will find all the cars,
all the traffic in the world.

Give him your granules, not your love,
a pound of confectioners.

He will move faster
than the recovering economy,
buying and selling, faster and faster:
lamps, watches, dental floss, condos,
whole agencies, fast enough to keep his place
in this world,
the world in its rightful place.

## THE APPRENTICE AT THE CHANCERY
(LUNCH HOUR)

The Apprentice thanks God
for his little friends, neuroses.
They keep him in line.

"Be glad and clap your hands
when you are alone," he tells himself.
"When else is it so clear
that you are not?"

He munches bananas
on the top of cliffside rocks,
flings his peels, random files,
to the trees below; branches—
like pastoral opportunities, sagging.

The sun is so bright,
it leaves teeth marks on his soul.

"More light," a dying Goethe said,
"I can still see."

# THE APPRENTICE AND THE EGG

Consider them,
so round and romantic,
perfect in every way.
They are what they are,
not some abstract,
oblong syllables of death.

No. They have taken up residence here—
in our houses, delighting in the space they use,
in their almost unobtrusive lifestyles.
(You can tell that by the way they stand
in the carton, the arabesque figure
each one cuts,
their almost military reserve.)

They stand against us.
(We are not their measurers!
We may have their pasts!)

So how shall the apprentice live then?

Sam Cooke will teach him
the cha-cha-cha.
He will go on tour: Seattle, Ashtabula,
do regional TV coffee klatches,
meet and discuss deep topics
with many women anchors.

He will learn how to give
successful halftime motivational speeches,
will make brief stops at 1600 Pa. Ave.:
the new cabinet member,
Minister of the Paleolithic,
chorus of the night.

## THE APPRENTICE ON VACATION

This is not Boca Raton or Spoon Harbor.
And the apprentice is not driving a mint blue
'64 Biscayne, slow, so he can hear the tread
talk to the road. He scoffs at whitewalls,
curb antennae.

The Apprentice goes with what he's got:
enough beans, jalapeños for chili,
the upstairs of an old firehouse, bare feet
and cable, a new woman to meet on Sunday.

This is quality of life.
This is socially redeeming Catholic Action:
breathe fire, drink beer.

Let the police sing on the sidewalks;
let the neighborhood arsonists,
all the crack-babies sing.

It's the least they could do.

## THE APPRENTICE BILOCATES

(A SECOND JOB)

The Apprentice's best days
canary the blue. He dances
under snow-white buds, rain
of calendar leaves.

He takes his delight in ladder marks
on the sides of houses,
in a well-drawn ceiling line!
He lunches on lawns: Big Macs, salted potatoes,
cokes like Cochise,
Rory Calhoun down the draw.

At night, in the spare upper reserves,
he can put his feet up
as his cousin talks about Kant.
He would listen, but the bases are so white
at the Jake, the grass so green.

It could be nineteen thirty-four again:
the apprentice could be his father,
as cumbersome, graceful men perform their rounds
in baggy, dusty uniforms,
shared outfield gloves.

All of that world is a stage
because it is set for nothing but itself:
a pearl under toothbrush lights—
heaven in its own way.

## THE APPRENTICE COUNSELS
## A NOT-SO-YOUNG RILKE

Li Po, drunk in his boat,
was every bit as foolish as you;
he could've been Curly, nyunk, nyukking his way
over the dark curtain, folds of eternity.

He had no audience but twin stars,
the only frogs of heaven.

Nothing could've gone wrong that night,
and the people he had to meet the next day
would've surely joined him in song
had he asked, loud as the approaching shore.

There is a moral in this exemplum,
for which I apologize—
but drink too!

Find a fat Germanic lass—to put in baldy,
someone who won't listen to a word you say.

# THE APPRENTICE SCOURS THE DIOCESE

The Apprentice sends out fliers,
wants to put a bid in on a nice
Franciscan woman: an advocate
of high fructose corn syrup, junkyard,
squatting oil pan discussions.

The two of them will spin West Virginia
Lambrusco, slices of pizza, whirly-bird,
in their hands. They would be Rousseaus-in-love,
wear the warm glove, silt of night ponds.
They would walk the county roads,
speak their stories beneath the rasp
and snap of autumnal corn.

She will smile, her face like the full moon,
above breasted hills, will call him—
nothing at all.

They will raise up a troupe of kids
onto city buses, a disturbance of tiny bare feet,
coins like Christmas in the farebox.

They will change the world.

THE APPRENTICE
# PHASE TWO

## MISPLACED YEARS

It is like the Apprentice had a camera
he didn't know how to work—
his whole family, a pantomime he's missed;
twenty years of memories, gone.
(He was in the bathroom!)

Pictures on his office wall should be a start,
but it's like his mind has been wiped by aliens.

E-mails tell him they are alive,
mug shots on Facebook, each
with slightly puzzled expression.

His life is a page he hasn't read; his children,
rumors. The Apprentice wants his money back,
a chance to try again—happy little people,
weapons around the Christmas tree.

He would rename them: Poppov, Guillermo,
Alexandrina.

But this is how it always is, no?
You get one day, make up the rest as you go.

# THE KIND OF (APPRENTICE) SEPTEMBER

The Apprentice's rollerblades gather dust
in what's left of the strawberries: life,
collapsing in the bed of its own making!

He'd wanted old banjos, deck evenings,
the gentle sway of Japanese lanterns;
Fictions should be coming over for the old haw-haw:
England and the Dardanelles.

But no; here his children barricade
inside their rooms, computing each future.
They see him clearly enough: two boys
called Eye-patch, a daughter, Heart Valve.

The sun sets in a backyard orange
liquor bottle. Grass and plastic table darken,
make for twilight as three dwarf pines, the alley,
begin to harbor night. He urges them
to read KARAMOZOV, to alphabetize!

He wants to hold each hand one more time,
before they leave his house—bereft,
for the running of their bulls.
He would squeeze each a half second too long,
just to give his last gift: his need,
insufficiency.

## SOMEWHERE ELSE

The Apprentice lives where no one knows
how to begin, or what language to use.
The sun and green leaves walk past
on great stork legs, oblivious
to the best he can do.

He is the sniffing dog they lead.

He is his parents' final say.

Oh, ragged remains, oh, impious thirsting;
who is more sober than the disquieted man?
Who sits closer to the window?

What can he give his children:
shards of Aztec, a rain dance?
They, too, will walk the corner store,
parent. They too will take this seat—
thirty years on.

His own mother spreads her under-the-bed
money—what she keeps from the government,
all over her small room: twenties on the sofa,
fifties, smoothed on the sill.

It's how we all pass our time—
working our assets, though our hearts,
surely, are somewhere else.

## THE APPRENTICE AS BOBBLEHEAD

The Apprentice wants horses, bloodlines,
a Rothschild bobblehead.
He wants a crust of the old upper.
He wants to sit on the polished curve of saddle,
say "round-a-lay."

His life, though, is a winter stream,
chiaroscuro: its blue-white treed banks
in a gallery window,
downtown Cleveland, forty years ago.

Every winter barks like a dog—empty, cold.
It gives us what we need.

The only answers we ever get
are for other people. We are
what is left of us, what we cannot find.
Drop the scratchy needle on the vein
of your choice: Franz Liszt, Lady Day.

There is no starch, no starfish here.

The Apprentice takes down his Capt. Crunch,
dies in the sound of spoon, empty bowl.

His wife, though, saves him, yet again.
She has a laugh for most occasions, gardens,
hosing grass, flowers, early in the morning—
as if she's onto something.

## POEM FOR APPRENTICE JUDE (DOWN'S)

His irises, more yellow than blue, startle,
wet porcelain face above the Canadian lake;
he looks back, past knocking moored boats,
toward a late sun.

He is as alien as anyone,
the mother lode: the given and your need to.

He won't tell me his name.

The Apprentice has seen the bus-stop kids,
how his son can only get outside their circle
because he doesn't talk well,
and so to his finger.

Maybe that's why it's "Dad, get off your ass,"
when I'm home—though the words aren't his:
"We've got a world to take the measure of":
unlined county roads on a scooter,
the next flavored smoothie; he chases
racquetballs—almost successfully.

This is what we do, because I didn't
see it again, because I so seldom do.
"Get off your ass, Dad. How much time
do you think we have?" Everything he can get
his hands on is adult gold, except gold,
which is yellow—like his eyes, telling me again
that this life, the one I work so badly
is really working me: greyhounds; that dewy web
which spans ground rock to garage—
how it swayed, wet, broken, this morning.

# THE APPRENTICE TAKES A SOAK

The Apprentice takes a soak with the Pardoner,
splitting hairs of a shirt neither will wear.
Petty thieves, they would be, surrounded
by objects d'art—30's garage sale wingtips,
bovine porcelain plates. They angle for pay:
Saturday lawn chairs, college football.

Creaking too violently, they rock for a mascot
to walk down the street.

On nearby hills, houses perch on fashionable ledges,
each person, dining amongst peerage.
The world is what it has created: its own poetry.

All crimes are not literary!

Chopin wanders Monsanto's corn: a poetic voice
no one hears—out loud, the place where we
are all going, the dirt we wear, the lies
we fashion.

Everyone pounds a drum for change!

All of them matter!

The Apprentice wants to inherit cracked earth.
He wants to feel the weight of his sins, wants them
to bring him all the way down,
into a sordid life, until his steps begin to speak
what must be said, one foot at a time.

## THE APPRENTICE SKUDS

The Apprentice searches for his consolation
before the pain. It saves time.
Why get operatic after all?
And what is beer for if not this?

Such is what passes for his suffering:
not the high road of the guttered;
but, rather, life from an excused distance.

(Fans, fans, all at a discount.
I slake, I wave!)

But how can the apprentice improve his mettle
through tomorrow's sins
today? Who can keep them away?

And so here he is, in this little boat
called time.

Come, hidden joys! Dance! There's room
enough! The frost is on the windowpane,
the plastic tree tinkles.
(Christmas children are coming!)

The Apprentice would be counted one:
this snail without a shell, lagging behind
as he does, skudding through the slow slime
of his life.

So how does he get Jesus to take him?

Already has.

## APPRENTICED IN PURGATORY

On the left bank, the Apprentice sits in waves
of grey grass—in breezes he cannot feel.
There are no stars in the grey sky,
no sky either.

Still, he has boats to fashion, signs to paint.

There is nothing here but the vast edges
drear and naked shingles of the world.

He will have to learn to live now,
where his body is.

He will let tomorrow, such as it will be,
take care of itself, as he foots ground,
runnels sand, waiting for guests.

This is the second start.

His arms, though, begin to moss,
his mouth as well. He feels a tail—
begin, its lengthening curl; scorpion now,
above him, he'd shadow himself
if a sun were to noon
above his head.

Defenses: he is, eyes and a hut,
just the one voice, Mumbles,
for company.

He must be the one that rises here—
though that effort
would split the goal.

## THE OAK STREET POLKA

He stands —against the pogrom
of time, even as God's world flutters in descent,
on broken, translucent wings:
a city of unremembered names.

Let the corrugation continue!
Let the greater substance have its way.

The Apprentice refuses to lament the passing
of this half-world. It spins, leaves
faster than he. If he runs quickly enough,
perhaps he can shed the surface of things.

Shall he praise the sky, after all,
for its lack of birds? Shall he praise the guitar
for its dusty sheath? Praise.
Praise! What else?

His children, after all, have grown
right out of his hand.

Praise be to the crop-duster! For He will toast us,
but not before a thorough shaking!
This is called death, little campers,
the horn of our going.

It blats across the countryside
in days which, finally, do not matter to anyone,
even to us; where there is nothing to do
but dance in the sunny tree box
you call your life.

# THE CALL

All pain is Christ's:
the raped, the flayed, the crucified—
the world's cities, crumbling into the stones
that gave them rise: Jerusalem, Athens,
Weirton.

We walk through lives
which do not lead us; through a bliss
we cannot stay.

Time is not for us.

It is a skate in the park,
if you take away the park—and the skates.

It's December 26<sup>th</sup>—all the packages
have been opened. (None were yours.)
You might call it surfeit,
this emptiness, though it was never that.

We walk though a world
which is almost world, touch it with hands
half-formed. Even our cries, voices
do not reach us. We continue,
waiting to be flesh, waiting to rise
into the pain which will make us real.

## THE APPRENTICE PAINTS HIS FACE

Like twenty miles of bad road,
he pounds each pothole,
hunts down struts, tires.

Scenery is a luxury he cannot afford.

Pray you don't meet him on a hot day,
along some sweaty lug nut roadside Utah—
all those Mormon faces
offering iced teas, their hat full of answers.

Part Ute, he knows the high
night terrain, the lights that shine
among the buttes: spirit guides, each
with gas station map in hand.
One points here, another there.
One makes a popping sound at the moon.

They know what they are doing.

He is so blessed, someone
should construct a monument: fifes and flowers,
rows of front-walk peonies
which bow at his every pass.

"Come gather, you flowers," he would say.
"Turn your heads hither.
I will cast my human petals;
I will slake your human tears!"

Great and holy hands press down
upon him daily: Isaiah in cut-offs—his audience,
every opaque Catholic Rosicrucianist—
each of them waving one kind
of ridiculous flag or another.

# THE APPRENTICE WASHES HIS HANDS

The Apprentice has loosed children
upon the world.

This could end badly!

Each got lost at the first turn, which is fitting
because their gifts do not matter here.
Their homes are memory. There is no place
for them on this or any other continent—
and their numbers grow: children without grace,
faces without regret. They will start a buzz
only they can hear. There will be no room for you
at that inn: roads will all be process; airplanes, ivy.

The Apprentice washes his hands
down to the elbows, prays in Aramaic
that their kingdom come.

His work is finished, so he clears off snow,
fires up the front yard grill. He cooks soy burgers
in mittens, enjoying his breath,
what remains of the neighborhood
as he waits for the Archbishop.

# THE APPRENTICE'S ASSIGNED PENANCE

is to write a poem about sloth.

He doesn't feel like it, would rather
eat dark green vegetables or practice his manners.

The prone figurine, the wan man,
horizontal, is too pale for lice.
What is his name, Ebenezer,
brother without intent? He needs a biography,
a reason for not being, taking up space—
or nearly so. Who will call him friend,
who will almost hold his hand?

He must claim him, his hypocrite heck-ler!
He must carry him like drapes, Marley armed,
each one becoming longer than it is! Pity him,
the heavy—without substance,
a weakened shadow. The Apprentice
does not want him, or himself.

He would throw down the gauntlet,
but his arms are in process.
(This fellow will not eat his vegetables.)
The Apprentice will not complete this task
until he works his way, as he did
when he was a teen, a pee-wee.

Any effort carries the name.

## APPRENTICE FAIL

Irony gently pirouettes,
turns his DNA like a porcelain figure
on a music box. Failure, a follower
in dummy's voice, throws him still:
"Hello, Robespierre. How long
do I have to keep speaking? . . ."

His doggie's name is Fail. His cat as well.
He sings for all the failures who've tried
to give themselves a different name.

He prays, "Mother of failures, protect me.
Save me from the claws of success, the harm
of fawning readers. Let not elaborate book deals
prevail upon me, the malice of auditoriums,
the green envy of disposable income."

There is no other way. Every success
is failure with nothing stamped on it—
the smaller the better.

Give the heathens their prizes: Pulitzer, Nobel,
MacArthur. Give me heaven
and your smile.

## THE APPRENTICE CONSIDERS THE PAST

It's no help—more backbone, humility:
illusions; the right-handed baseball mitt,
no good.

Amends to youthful friends, gone
beyond repair, who will not be here
when he is, again, fed: a wrinkled babe,
his options.

Which day could he set right?

So he must gather his students,
refashion the coast of Australia!

Divinity, elsewhere, works
amid the green shelves of happier leaves,
undying tears. (The Apprentice insists
he has a heart there.)

"Stay here as long as you need to,"
the voices will say. "Things will not clear
until you are ready."

Repentance is a long road.

It opened its eyes before you did.

## THE APPRENTICE WINS THE TEACHING AWARD

Thankfully, it happens on its own—
through the windows: winter wood taking back
parsed light, concrete block, paint.
Books are cut from that fiber, after all,
carry hints of the first philosophy.

Students can smell the only foolishness
worth anything: through snowy trees.
Wallace Stevens is out there, talking to himself,
next to snow-pated stone goblins, ginkgoes, coyotes.

Cliffs at the edge of campus overlook the Ohio,
and though you can't enter that rock,
you can wait your turn.

We never live here.

There's too much missing.

So we peck among the dead, roll them over,
search their pockets. All their coins, halved.

We could just stand (and sit) here in class.
That would be more honest.

We call this moment the poem.
Dress it anyway we like.

## THE APPRENTICE, TROLLED

He gets it—too late: the danger in knowing
more than he does.

Kicked out of a club he'd wanted to start,
he is left over-extended,
half of what he never was.

And it's hard to give thanks—
for shame, to dance with no one, limping
(a whole world of yesterdays).

Come children, gather around and listen
to the fail that is your portion, cup.

No one will notice
because no one expected more.

The world has seen you clearly enough.

Call it a postcard,
a message from home.

The sensible march freely—obedient.
Granted, it's a small army, but there is no battle;
at least none you will direct.

## HUMILITY MEETS STUPID

The Apprentice was not made for this world,
sits on top of it like Buddha—
or some condensation,
foldering his pipe, lost in scenarios
which matter to no one.

How does food even come this man's way?

How is he free to walk to the corner store?

Who is watching him?

These are miracles beyond comprehension.

Thankfully, though, his world gets smaller
by the day—until everything
becomes someone else's concern.

He folds his wings, not to fly
into this sunset, or any other. He must
become a nose in the air, sniffing. . . .

Nothing, he will put on new shoes,
take to streets he will not know.
People will start to appear
with real faces. There will be a new commerce,
without abstractions. France will be the flag
he waves, a blessing.

## THE APPRENTICE AS DISMUS

He lifts each Infant:
church crèches, empty as time.
It's how he gets the 6 o'clock news,
lining them up on 4<sup>th</sup>, early Sunday mornings;
fifty votive candles
flagging the darkened meters.

He ties black babies, bloody dolls,
to fences surrounding Planned Parenthood.

Christmas Christians are appalled.

Work day done, he pays the mailman
to do those rounds, unwind.
After beers, he's home again, lining up
his shoes, checking the bagged placenta
he keeps in the meat drawer.

Dietrich Bonhoeffer rolls over in his grave—
finding, the Apprentice hopes,
a measure of comfort.

There is none here.

## THE GUERILLAS OF LOVE

Apprentices, masked, attack a nursing home,
quartered oranges in hand.
They confound power at its every turn,

erect "Jesus died here" tin signs
on mounds of city dump—which waver,
warbling in the wind. (One Confessional box
sits a-Tardis, on the slant.)

As priests, they march lockstep, in shades,
through the shopping mall, each carrying
an oversized Margaret Sanger on his back.

They sing hymns outside public schools,
carrying signs of distorted children,
until they are policed away, hum,
"Where has all the money gone, long time passing?
Where has all the money gone, long time ago? . . ."

They lay sleeves of thorns on random graves,
broken TV sets at intersections, Tuesday evenings.

Does it help?

No.

# THE APPRENTICE PRAYS WITH D. A. LEVY

## PART 1

The Apprentice keys the Bishop's Caddy.

Back home, Emily rocks the creaking porch,
offers the Apprentice a ribboned snow shovel:
"This is my introduction."

d. a. levy, for his part, smokes a cigarette, says less—
all the time. Why do Catholics always feed on themselves,
he wonders from the stoop? Give him wintery Cleveland
in 1965: a wasteland and its want as a way to speak truth—
that there is no completion here, ever.

Nothing is certain—except the death that sums us:
this beat city, every empty street, early Broadway, Collinwood.
There was little illusion in '65, about how much you mattered,
about what you could bring to any situation.

That was the tangible truth, without Catholic or Ginsberg
Buddhist exemplars. People in the then were, for him, real—
in their suffering, in the scraps of paper that swirled
the only nightlife down East 9th.

It was like a Browns game: incompleteness
filling the stands, in the crowded after. It was
in what the partial share; why people the Apprentice
didn't know could howl and be understood: the Dog Pound
was life; football, a means. Nobody cared about what lay beyond
because of the truth they all almost carried. Not like
at the Catholic Institute where love is cold, thin,
paper-centered. Levy and the city, they were what mattered:
dogs without their bones.

Dickinson sits down on the sidewalk in snow pants,
smokes a Lucky. It's all true. She'll give him that:
levy and his East Cleveland.

The only truth is want.

## PART 2

The Apprentice does Chaplin—in tweed:
an aging dusty dancing bear at the head of the class.
But where are all the Beat Bishoprics,
the levys, he wants to know? Maybe in learned East Coast—
homeless shelters, where no one gives a Dante double fig
about your degrees, or your take on the liturgy.

There is no mission here. Who are you going to be nice to?
The street guy, so he can stop playing the fool
to get his biscuit, too much of your philosophy?

If levy were alive today he would he be spraying paint poems
on the stanchions of the Carnegie Bridge. Indoors,
it would be dim apartments, greasy kitchen walls.

He would never come clean.

Catholics lie the loudest, because all they possess
are their answers. (It's in a pamphlet on Fatima.)

Come back, levy, the Church needs you, though you
cannot save us, Prince of Nothing, part of no community
that matters. The Apprentice needs to work against—
resting places. He needs to live his life in a shiver,
where no thought is complete, no friend near enough
to change.

He must rage each silent night.

His calm is his fight.

## PART 3

Miss Dickinson assents, demurs.
The only real people are homeless, yes.
But where there is only dirt
there is possibility. She would weed and plant,
say hello to a neighbor—a cup or a thimble:
it's up to you.

Most days she can just sit
on her small Ohio Valley back porch, rock,
hands on her lap as she watches cars
whiz by on Route 7.

A butterfly could find its way here—
or the end of your days.

For God's sake, she wants to say, Shelley
has been dead—for longer than he knew.
Most days pass calmly into the next.

Do something with your hands.

(Percy worshipped youth—flourish
and undergrowth.)

Give your pennies to the poor,
but know they won't help *them* very much.

We all wait, ignorance itself, trying to correct
our steps, using the past as sortilege.

She would advise no further.

She would say what has been said.

## MISS DICKINSON ANSWERS HIGGINSON AND
## *THE ATLANTIC MONTHLY*

The Apprentice holds her hand as they walk,
like a couple of kids who wait
for the world to catch up.

It never does.

Let them have their time.
We will wait where birds sing
and spring snow-water runs down the drive.

Call it interlude, or every life
without an answer. We wait, instructed,
for what will come—

Eucharist: the world, finally, on our tongues,
eating and being eaten; not like now,
but pure, maintaining the shape
we give away to everyone we meet—conduits,
stained glass windows, the fire of God.

"We are jackdaws, ostentation
made flesh, a too energetic response in dashes,
blue piqué shawls."

THE APPRENTICE
# PHASE THREE

## THE APPRENTICE AND THE CHRIST

The Apprentice breaks up wet, rotting planks,
one after another in the woods—for no reason,
watching the soaked fibers shred, the bugs.
He notices Jesus, walking into view.

He'd smile at his Maker, but there's nothing
to his effort—again. He's in the middle,
with all his force.

And what does His Lord do?
With one touch He could make the world
real, change the dense to forest,
brighten the sky. But He does not.

He sits on the ground, gathers
His robe; He leans back a little,
without saying His Word. He gazes up
at the sky, waiting for the Apprentice
to tear though his wood, apparently,
to work up his sweat.

And the Apprentice goes right on, not quite
to speed, knowing that this must end,
hoping that it will be soon.

## JESUS ON THE STREET

The Apprentice meets Jesus: His hair,
greased, stringy, bobbing in front of His face.
He dances, a little crazy, inverted-like,
on the sidewalk.

There is no music the Apprentice can hear—
but that is nothing new.

Jesus offers him a pull of Jack, invites him
into a bar, so dark that he can't see
anyone for months, which is a good thing
because the dim contortionists
all wear versions of his happy face.

Jesus laughs.
"You worry too much.
Great minds are gifts, but not the giver. . . .
Try the stuffed mushrooms."

Neon and streetlight create the small window;
old pool players materialize. A time gone,
and the time before that.
Jesus leads him outside for a smoke,
sets His Stroh's down.

"I could do another miracle if you'd like.
Raise the dead.

I will."

## LOCUTION POEM

Splashing through the waters
of inattention—a lengthening of shadows,
what pilgrim could accept *this*:
fictions becoming truth, illusory people, pieces
on an illusory chessboard!

It's embarrassing.

> *For whom?*

So there is no scandal for You?
These splatterings on the wall, these triumphant
priests in high places, the sluice that opens;
these do not grieve?

> *I am peace.*

> *Everything that is, comes from me.*
> *The sky's blue, its Easter seal.*
> *Live where I am.*

> *You already do.*

> *Don't waste your time, energy—.*
> *These are what you have to give.*

But the pilgrim's hands are full
of broken toys: time,
purgatory on wheels, a slow succession
of lives not lived,
spiritual whimpery . . .

Okay . . . I get it:

This is the speed I go—
because this is the speed I am.
No velocity is better than another.
There are reasons why I languish,
and they are yours.

But there is a heaven, too,
and less. And who wants to be that—
while winds creak summer limbs
so open that they might be
a new life?

*That's your word: "less."*

*Everything will be worked out—
to your joy.*

*Everyone has his own turning.*

But the mockery: those small,
untimely deaths,
the almost-voices?

*You know words, and Therese.
Little flowers live
where they can best grow,
where the sun takes their measures,
where rain waits.
Who would not stoop to see, hear
each play unfold?*

Then why do I feel this disdain
for miniaturization, for floating carcasses,
this craving to be more?

And why are there typhoons?

*Because you do not yet see.*

Okay, okay. You are here. . . .
Can we set up a final shop,
adopt a puppy?

*No.*

ം ം ം ം

How do I beat pride,
that wooden monkey, anyway?

*You don't.*

So I mis-take, gathering all my time,
what glitters, when what I should do
is turn inward, into the songs of birds?

*(No answer.)*

And the gray phasing of lukewarmness,
making its ugly rounds:
how do I beat that tired monster?

*That's just you—alone.*
*You don't have to be.*
*Am I not here?*

But is there any way to hurry
this step, this wayward slough of mediocrity?
Is there any way to get heaven now,
the portion of it that be assignable?

Or is that just the Yeats in us,
that which would make heroic
the throat of a frog in a ditch?

We want this time to matter
because this is where we spend it,
in our waking, talking,
in the eating of cheese.

It does count, but not by your eyes.

And so here we are again, in the flight

*which is . . .*
*the song that sings you.*

*You do not have to make the world*
*larger, or fill it with air—*

*unless it be sweet. . . . Sing time.*
*I find consolation there:*
*leaves blowing past, their colors—*
*like the seasons.*

And so we must wait, engage—
without all these little flags?

*Yes. . . . If you do not listen,*
*you will not hear.*

*And you are not sitting on your chair*
*for yourself alone.*

*Sing each day—*
*in a chorus whose absolute music*
*you cannot yet hear.*

# NOTES

## PHASE ONE

**COME, NEGAGFOK**

Negagfok is the Inuit spirit that likes cold and stormy weather. GREEN ACRES was a TV series that starred Arnold Ziffel, a pig.

I have no idea about Rilke's laundry woman—only that domesticity rests for no man, not even for an aristocratic one.

**CHRISTMAS WITH ED AND THE REMOTE CONTROL**

Loretta Swit played Hot Lips on the MASH TV series.

**THE APPRENTICE REJOICES**

Columbo was an absent-minded TV detective who would flail his arms around while obliquely linking up the telling evidence, all of course, to the great annoyance of his brilliant, guilty adversary, who had to stand there and take it—the show's hour almost up.

Cuchulain is a character from the Ulster Cycle in Irish mythology. In Yeats' most famous poem about him, he is spelled into battling the sea after having unknowingly slain his own son.

## THE APPRENTICE SEES HIMSELF IN THE SUNSET

Carmen Miranda was a fetching South American Hollywood movie star who used to sing and dance with great mounds of fruit on her head.

Jimmy Swaggart was a noted TV evangelist and cousin of Jerry Lee Lewis. He was caught on several occasional with prostitutes (of the golden heart), probably for mutual counseling.

The flowers bring to mind the old 60's TV commercial where hippie-types, arm in arm, sang: "I'd like to buy the world a Coke, and keep it company," followed by something about "apple trees and honey bees and snow-white turtle doves." Today the company does much the same at movies, telling us that "Coke is happiness."

Alan Iverson was a diminutive assassin who played in the NBA. He was famous for his lightning quick cross-over dribble, a move which surely confounded any still living referee from the 50s—a time before black people and athletic creativity had been invented.

Turning one's head and coughing was standard right-of-passage procedure for the first day of football practice many years ago— the doctor's way of testing would-be players for hernias (and courage?).

## THE APPRENTICE CONSIDERS FLEAS

The Ayatollah Khomeini was Jimmy Carter's holy (Batman) bane in the late 70s.

## THE APPRENTICE AND THE EGG

Sam Cooke was a smooth as silk pop singer in the 60s. One of his hits was "Everybody Likes to Do the Cha Cha Cha."

### THE APPRENTICE BILOCATES

Cochise was a popular Apache chief in the westerns of the 50s and 60s. Rory Calhoun was a leading man in many of them. He wore a pompadour haircut with the small patch of grey up high. Never understood that, maybe something about the gift of maturity—with a pompadour. (Where would we be without Hollywood?)

The Jake was Jacobs field in Cleveland.

### THE APPRENTICE COUNSELS A NOT-SO-YOUNG RILKE

Li Po was an 8th century Chinese poet who supposedly fell off his boat and drowned while either leaning into his drunken reflection or trying to embrace the wavering moon (the middle one). Curly was the most profound of the Three Stooges.

## PHASE TWO

### THE APPRENTICE TAKES A SOAK

Monsanto is a huge agri-business who many foreign countries will not allow to operate within their borders. President Obama (or was it George Bush) seemed to do everything he could to pressure said countries into allowing that company to operate freely, an odd occurrence given both the Left's disdain for the 1% and their purported love for sensible ecology.

The truth about American politicians: "If their lips are moving, they're lying." (Or, in the case of First Ladies: "If her lips are moving, he's lying.")

### THE APPRENTICE, TROLLED

Getting trolled on the internet is basically getting played. The victim's pride does him in. He thinks he knows something, has much to say about a subject which the world would do well to hear. The "partner/stranger" plays along, slowly aggravating, taking the knower in until the victim's puffed up self-image is made plain to the four people who are still paying attention. (My son insists that St. Paul was the first troll. Arrested by Pharisees and Sadducees after Jesus's death, he caused a riot in the temple by loudly insisting that he believed in the resurrection from the dead. In that particular case, David tells me, the Romans played the role of the moderator by "locking the thread.")

## THE APPRENTICE AS DISMUS

Planned Parenthood was begun by Margaret Sanger, who wanted to get rid of undesirables: blacks, Jews, soldiers, immigrants, indigents, and the mentally ill. The irony is that black American leaders have so embraced her perspective.

Dietrich Bonhoeffer was hung for trying to assassinate Hitler.

## THE GUERILLAS OF LOVE

Dr. Who's Tardis is shaped like a Confessional box.

## THE APPRENTICE PRAYS WITH D. A. LEVY
## PART 1

When Higginson (who recommended she not publish) visited Dickinson for the first time in Amherst, she nervously made her way across the ample first floor room, put a few day lilies in his hand, telling him, "These are my introduction."

Levy was a fine Beat poet from Cleveland who killed himself in the late 60s—maybe so he wouldn't have to take a poet-in-residence job at Wisconsin. (He did have a great and justified suspicion of position.)

The Dog Pound is (and has been) the rowdy end of Cleveland's stadiums during Browns football games—since the Minnifield, Dixon days. Great camaraderie can be found there, less personal illusion perhaps.

**PART 2**

Dante's double fig was basically a case of flipping God a two-handed bird. (Paul Mariani does a nice contemporary rendition in "Quid Pro Quo.")

## MISS DICKINSON ANSWERS HIGGINSON AND *THE ATLANTIC MONTHLY*

The aforementioned master critic Higginson worked for TAM as some sort of expert in poetry.

# PHASE THREE

## JESUS AND THE STREET

Jack is Jack Daniels. Stroh's is, or used to be a favorite beer at Madden's Irish Village in Cleveland.

www.ingramcontent.com/pod-product-compliance
Lightning Source LLC
LaVergne TN
LVHW021621080426
835510LV00019B/2697